M000158438

BELIEVE AND ACHIEVE

summersdale

BELIEVE AND ACHIEVE

Copyright © Summersdale Publishers Ltd, 2022

All rights reserved.

Compiled by Stephanie Buick

No part of this book may be reproduced by any means, nor transmitted, nor translated into a machine language, without the written permission of the publishers.

Condition of Sale
This book is sold subject to the condition that it shall not, by way of trade or otherwise, be lent, resold, hired out or otherwise circulated in any form of binding or cover other than that in which it is published and without a similar condition including this condition being imposed on the subsequent purchaser.

An Hachette UK Company
www.hachette.co.uk

Summersdale Publishers Ltd
Part of Octopus Publishing Group Limited
Carmelite House
50 Victoria Embankment
LONDON
EC4Y 0DZ
UK

www.summersdale.com

Printed and bound in China

ISBN: 978-1-80007-392-0

Substantial discounts on bulk quantities of Summersdale books are available to corporations, professional associations and other organizations. For details contact general enquiries: telephone: +44 (0) 1243 771107 or email: enquiries@summersdale.com.

To...

From...

Go boldly and honestly through the world. Learn to love the fact that there is nobody else quite like you.

Daniel Radcliffe

Believe in yourself and you will be unstoppable

Create the highest, grandest vision possible for your life because you become what you believe.

Oprah Winfrey

FIND OUT WHO YOU ARE AND DO IT ON PURPOSE.

Dolly Parton

TURN YOUR
DREAMS
INTO GOALS
AND THEY
WILL BECOME
REALITY

If you don't like something, change it. If you can't change it, change your attitude.

Maya Angelou

A champion is defined not by their wins but how they can recover when they fall.

Serena Williams

Let your
self-belief
fuel your
ambitions

You don't have to see the whole staircase, just take the first step.

Martin Luther King Jr

If you hear a voice
within you say,
"I cannot paint",
then by all means
paint and that voice
will be silenced.

Vincent van Gogh

Choose success every day

If something is important enough, even if the odds are stacked against you, you should still do it.

Elon Musk

Progress always involves risk; you can't steal second base and keep your foot on first.

Frederick B. Wilcox

BE YOUR OWN OWN GREATEST CHEERLEADER

**Courage is
very important.
Like a muscle,
it is strengthened
by use.**

Ruth Gordon

Make bold choices and make mistakes. It's all those things that add up to the person you become.

Angelina Jolie

START HERE; GO ANYWHERE

The formula of happiness and success is just being actually yourself, in the most vivid possible way you can.

Meryl Streep

A winner is a dreamer who never gives up.

Nelson Mandela

Obstacles are the stepping stones of your journey to success

A hero is an ordinary individual who finds the strength to persevere and endure in spite of overwhelming obstacles.

Christopher Reeve

THE KEY TO SUCCESS IS TO START BEFORE YOU'RE READY.

Marie Forleo

STAND
AS TALL AS
YOU WANT
TO FEEL

Do what you were born to do. You just have to trust yourself.

Beyoncé

If it doesn't challenge you, it doesn't change you.

Fred DeVito

Fuel your plans with action and make your dreams come true

The most effective way to do it is to do it.

Amelia Earhart

There will
be obstacles.
There will
be doubters.
There will
be mistakes.
But with hard
work… there
are no limits.

Michael Phelps

You have
unlimited
potential

**Change is hard
at first, messy
in the middle
and so glorious
at the end.**

Robin Sharma

Giving up
can never ever
be an option.

Greta Thunberg

YOU ARE
SO MUCH
STRONGER
THAN YOU
THINK

**Excellence
is not a skill.
It is an
attitude.**

Ralph Marston

If you work really hard and you're kind, amazing things will happen.

Conan O'Brien

YES
YOU
CAN!

The only time
you run out
of chances is
when you stop
taking them.

Anonymous

Success is a state of mind. If you want success, start thinking of yourself as a success.

Joyce Brothers

Be your own kindest critic

The truth is
nobody knows
what's inside
of you... Only
you know what you
can accomplish
and what you
are capable of.

Jennifer Lopez

THERE'S NO DREAM THAT IS TOO BIG.

Lady Gaga

WITH HUGE
HOPES AND
HARD WORK,
ANYTHING IS
POSSIBLE

If you want to succeed as much as you want to breathe, then you will be successful.

Eric Thomas

Small opportunities are often the beginning of great enterprises.

Demosthenes

You can
achieve
anything
you put
your
mind to

Say it, believe it, work for it and pray for it.

Elaine Thompson-Herah

We must have
perseverance
and above all
confidence in
ourselves.
We must believe
that we are gifted
for something and
that this thing
must be attained.

Marie Curie

Self-belief is your first step to success

You can, you should, and if you're brave enough to start, you will.

Stephen King

It isn't where
you came from,
it's where you're
going that counts.

Ella Fitzgerald

HOPE
IS THE
HEARTBEAT
OF THE
SOUL

With confidence, you have won even before you have started.

Marcus Garvey

Believe in yourself. Even if you don't, pretend you do and at some point you will.

Venus Williams

THERE
ARE NO
BARRIERS,
ONLY
BRIDGES

You need to
put your heart
into making a
difference.

Stevie Wonder

Optimism is essential to achievement and it is also the foundation of courage.

Nicholas Murray Butler

One foot in front of the other – you will get there

Life has
got all those
twists and turns.
You've got to
hold on tight
and off you go.

Nicole Kidman

DO NOT FEAR MISTAKES; THERE ARE NONE.

Miles Davis

YOU HAVE
THE POWER
TO GET
WHERE YOU
WANT TO BE

A lot of people are afraid to say what they want. That's why they don't get what they want.

Madonna

**Ambition
is a dream
with a
V8 engine.**

Elvis Presley

Push
forward,
persevere
and be
patient

It's amazing what you can get if you quietly, clearly and authoritatively demand it.

Meryl Streep

Some of your
greatest pains
become your
greatest
strengths.

Drew Barrymore

Dream hard, work harder

Believe that life is worth living and your belief will help create the fact.

William James

If you can't fly,
run; if you can't
run, walk; if you
can't walk, crawl;
but by all means
keep moving.

Martin Luther King Jr

MAKE YOUR COMEBACK STRONGER THAN YOUR SETBACK

Embrace the glorious mess that you are.

Elizabeth Gilbert

**Never take
your eye off
that winding
road you have
paved by being
courageously you.**

Chrissy Metz

YOU
CAN
AND
YOU
WILL

The secret to
getting ahead is
getting started.

Anonymous

Excellence is an art won by training and habituation.

Aristotle

The strength within you is greater than the task ahead

You can do anything
you want, even if
you are being told
negative things.
Stay strong and
find motivation.

Misty Copeland

JUST BE YOURSELF. THERE IS NO ONE BETTER.

Taylor Swift

NOTHING GREAT EVER CAME THAT EASY

All our dreams can come true if we have the courage to pursue them.

Walt Disney

Sometimes you only need a little nudge to become something you could have never imagined.

Marcus Rashford

Let your
faith in
yourself
be stronger
than your
fears

There are
no regrets in life,
just lessons.

Jennifer Aniston

Fear is going
to be a player
in your life
but you get to
decide how much.

Jim Carrey

Follow what sets your soul alight

It is not the mountain we conquer but ourselves.

Edmund Hillary

You only get
one go at life,
which is thrilling.
Only you can make
yourself into who
you want to be.

Joanna Lumley

THINK BIG,
THINK BOLD,
THINK BRAVE

It is hard to fail,
but it is worse
never to have
tried to succeed.

Theodore Roosevelt

Success is liking yourself, liking what you do and liking how you do it.

Maya Angelou

YOU CAN
ACCOMPLISH
ANYTHING

As soon as you
trust yourself,
you will know
how to live.

Johann
Wolfgang von Goethe

**There is
no limitation
to what you
can achieve.**

Lailah Gifty Akita

This is
just the
beginning

What you get by
achieving your
goals is not
as important as
what you become
by achieving
your goals.

Zig Ziglar

THERE ISN'T A SINGLE PATH TO SUCCESS – THERE ARE MANY.

Deborah Meaden

GIVE YOURSELF PERMISSION TO GROW

**Being brave
isn't the absence
of fear. Being
brave is having
that fear but
finding a way
through it.**

Bear Grylls

I can't be a
product; no one
can do that to
me... I have
power over
everything I do.

Adele

Your positive
intentions
will lead
to positive
outcomes

No matter where you're from, your dreams are valid.

Lupita Nyong'o

Take chances,
make mistakes.
That's how
you grow.

Mary Tyler Moore

Your first step to success lies within you

**Accept who
you are; and
revel in it.**

Morrie Schwartz

Aim high, work hard
and care deeply
about what you
believe in...
And when you're
knocked down, get
right back up.

Hillary Clinton

A LITTLE
PROGRESS
EACH DAY
LEADS TO
GREAT
ACHIEVEMENTS

When you are required to exhibit strength, it comes.

Joseph Campbell

Feet, what do I need them for if I have wings to fly?

Frida Kahlo

TRUST
YOURSELF
AND MAKE
IT HAPPEN

If something
stands between
you and your
success – move it.
Never be denied.

Dwayne Johnson

If one advances confidently in the direction of his dreams... he will meet with a success unexpected in common hours.

Henry David Thoreau

Look
the world
straight
in the eye

I think
nothing's more
alluring than
confidence.

Margot Robbie

DO NOT DARE NOT TO DARE.

C. S. Lewis

TAKE
A STEP.
MOVE
CLOSER TO
YOUR GOAL.
REPEAT.

Your own resolution to succeed is more important than any other one thing.

Abraham Lincoln

Only those who dare to fail greatly can ever achieve greatly.

Robert F. Kennedy

Obstacles
are your
opportunity
to learn
and grow

Success is a science; if you have the conditions, you get the result.

Oscar Wilde

The distance
is nothing;
it is only the
first step that
is difficult.

Madame du Deffand

Celebrate your strengths

The beautiful thing about learning is that no one can take it away from you.

B. B. King

The dictionary
is the only
place where
success comes
before work.

Stubby Currence

DO WHAT YOU LOVE AND LOVE WHAT YOU DO

No one can make you feel inferior without your consent.

Eleanor Roosevelt

**Be yourself.
An original
is always
worth more
than a copy.**

Suzy Kassem

BEGIN
EACH DAY
WITH FIRE
IN YOUR
BELLY

Inspiration comes from within yourself. One has to be positive. When you're positive, good things happen.

Deep Roy

**The greater
the difficulty,
the more glory
in surmounting it.**

Epictetus

Wake up determined; go to sleep satisfied

If you truly pour
your heart into
what you believe,
even if it makes
you vulnerable,
amazing things can
and will happen.

Emma Watson

YOUR LIFE BELONGS TO YOU AND YOU ALONE.

Chimamanda Ngozi Adichie

FILL YOUR LIFE WITH PURPOSE, PASSION AND POSITIVITY

Success is the sum of small efforts, repeated day in and day out.

Robert Collier

The only courage you ever need is the courage to fulfil the dreams of your own life.

Oprah Winfrey

Let today's disappointment become tomorrow's determination

Expect problems and eat them for breakfast.

Alfred A. Montapert

Power means
happiness.
Power means
hard work
and sacrifice.

Beyoncé

Your courage is greater than your doubts

However bad
life may seem,
there is always
something you
can do and
succeed at.

Stephen Hawking

No matter who
you are, no matter
what you did,
no matter where
you've come from,
you can always...
become a better
version of yourself.

Madonna

DON'T LIMIT YOUR CHALLENGES – CHALLENGE YOUR LIMITS

Action is the foundational key to all success.

Pablo Picasso

Don't compare your progress to other people. We are all different.

Joe Wicks

GO FOR IT!

Success means
having the courage,
the determination
and the will to
become the person
you believe you
were meant to be.

George Sheehan

**Optimism
is the faith
that leads to
achievement.**

Helen Keller

Be determined in your goals and flexible in your strategy

Don't give up trying
what you really
want to do.
Where there is love
and inspiration,
I don't think you
can go wrong.

Ella Fitzgerald

BE YOURSELF. TAKE CONTROL OF YOUR LIFE.

Emma Bunton

GREAT
THINGS
HAVE SMALL
BEGINNINGS

Trust yourself. You know more than you think you do.

Benjamin Spock

When you have a dream, you've got to grab it and never let go.

Carol Burnett

Are you ready to blaze a trail to the stars?

Listen to your truths, desires and wants... Believe you deserve all of it.

Whoopi Goldberg

Every struggle
in your life has
shaped you into
the person you are
today. Be thankful
for the hard times
– they can only
make you stronger.

Keanu Reeves

There is no magic to achievement. It's really about hard work, choices and persistence.

Michelle Obama

BELIEVE
AND
ACHIEVE

Have you enjoyed this book?
If so, find us on Facebook at
Summersdale Publishers, on Twitter
at @Summersdale and on Instagram
at @summersdalebooks and get in
touch. We'd love to hear from you!

www.summersdale.com